Boost Your Confidence to Excel in School
(College and University Edition)
By Jean Young

EXPERIENCE
EVERYTHING
P U B L I S H I N G

Disclaimer

This document is geared towards providing exact and reliable information in regards to the topic and issue covered. The publication is sold with the idea that the publisher is not required to render accounting, officially permitted, or otherwise, qualified services. If advice is necessary, legal or professional, a practiced individual in the profession should be ordered.

- From a Declaration of Principles which was accepted and approved equally by a Committee of the American Bar Association and a Committee of Publishers and Associations:

The information provided herein is stated to be truthful and consistent, in that any liability, in terms of inattention or otherwise, by any usage or abuse of any policies, processes, or directions contained within is the solitary and utter responsibility of the recipient reader. Under no circumstances will any legal responsibility or blame be held against the publisher for any reparation, damages, or monetary loss due to the information herein, either directly or indirectly.

The information herein is offered for informational purposes solely, and is universal as so. The presentation of the information is without contract or any type of guarantee assurance.

The trademarks that are used are without any consent, and the publication of the trademark is without permission or backing by the trademark owner. All trademarks and brands within this book are for clarifying purposes only and are the owned by the owners themselves, not affiliated with this document.

Introduction

Being supremely self-confident is not something that you need to have to be happy in life. There is no right or wrong when it comes to how much confidence a person must have just like there is no right or wrong when it comes to how we view a glass: is it half-empty or half-full? Whether you have self-confidence, lack self-confidence or even have no self-confidence at all is totally fine. It is not a wrong way to be if that is how you prefer to be. However, it might be worth noting that possessing a good level of confidence is going to be very helpful for you when it comes to achieving your goals and being successful.

So why is it important to be confident? Overall, it is easier to be happy in life when you are confident and you are more likely to succeed as well. Below are several other benefits of being a confident person.

1. When you are confident, you also have a high sense of self-worth and you also believe in your capabilities and your skills. As a result, you have a higher self-esteem and you are proud of who you are and what you have accomplished.
2. Because you are happier when you are confident, it also results in being able to enjoy more what life has to offer.
3. Doubting yourself and your abilities is a mental torture we do not want to go through. But if we lack self-confidence, we are always making ourselves undergo this kind of torture. Thus, a person who is confident is free from self-doubt.
4. Confidence has a great influence on how powerful and strong you feel. When a challenge comes along, it is easier for you to overcome them because you feel empowered that you can do it.
5. When you are confident, you do not allow yourself to give in to the anxiety and fear that you get when a new challenge arises. You rise up to the challenge knowing that you can deal with it and accept whatever happens.
6. Because a confident person often does not have to deal with as much fear, anxiety, self-doubt and all the other negative feelings that come hand in hand with lack or no self-confidence, you are most likely to have lesser stress and it is easier to obtain a peace of mind.
7. You'll have more energy and motivation to accomplish any goal because you are confident that you can do it.
8. It is easier to interact with others.
9. If you consider think about the effects of no/less anxiety, fear and self-doubt added to more peace of mind, less stress and better rest then you can surely come up with the conclusion that your body will be in a healthier state.
10. Confident people have a higher rate of success over those who lack self-confidence or do not have any confidence at all.

To sum it all up, having low self-confidence is going to weaken you over time. It is normal for people with confidence issues to feel like they cannot be good at things or that they cannot handle any challenging situations. They fear that they might get rejected so in order to avoid the risk of being rejected, they decide to stay right where they are and miss out on great opportunities. Or if they do decide to go out there and take the risk, rejection is going to be a nightmare for them. This only increases the fear of rejection. And if this cycle happens over and over again, you are eventually going to weaken yourself.

On the other hand, when you are confident about yourself, being rejected is not enough to turn you off from applying to the different colleges or universities that you are trying to get into. You know that you will be able to handle rejections well, if you do get rejected and will be able to come back even stronger. So being a confident person is going to be worth it because of how much you can benefit from it, as stated earlier.

So now that you are done with high school, it is time for you to move on to the next level of education which is enrolling yourself in a college or university. There are some things that you need to remember though.

Even though your knowledge, skills and talent can take you a long way, many would still consider confidence as an essential when it comes to accomplishing things. And when you do succeed as a result of your confidence in yourself, it is also easy for you to enjoy your success.

When you are in college or just about to go to college, what are the things that you need to look out for that could have an effect on your confidence level?

- The feedback that your instructor or professor gives can affect your confidence level. A professor that shows concern for your future or one that provides feedback that is positive can help boost your confidence level. However, professors who provide criticisms may not be good for your confidence level.
- If you encounter difficult obstacles in your path, it is easy to get discouraged and lose confidence in yourself. But when you have a strong support system composed of your friends, family and mentors that you can count on in this trying times. When you feel like giving up, look up to them for motivations and inspirations to boost your confidence and get going. A good support system can help boost your confidence but not having one is going to decrease your confidence level even further.
- When you start giving in to your doubts, fear and anxiety, you start losing your confidence in yourself and your abilities. But if you tell yourself that you will succeed because you can, you are greatly boosting your confidence when it comes to succeeding.

When you enter the college life, you can also expect the problems that you encounter to be more complicated. However, you need to keep hanging in there and keep the confidence in order to succeed. What are the different things that you can do in order to boost your confidence and do well in this stage of your life? Well, read on to find out!

Comparing Confidence of College Students Then And Now

SAT scores may have decreased over time. However, more and more college students claim or see themselves as being above average. A researcher says that the generation that we have now prefers the image of success over the actual success.

In research that was done by in the US reports that the biggest changes that could be seen in the college students of today and the past generations is the self-confidence of the students. Other things that also increased include the abilities in leadership and public speaking. The drive to succeed in college students have also increased.

If you compare the grades of college students, there were only around 19% of college students that got an A- or A+ in 1966. However, that number has increased to 48% in 2009. This could be a reason why many students consider themselves to be above average.

Confidence is good but too much is bad. It can also lead to bloated egos and narcissism which is more common nowadays. The line has to be drawn when it comes to the right amount of confidence to avoid being too self-centered.

Section 1: Say No To Your Little Voice

Regardless of the stage in life that we are at, there will always be that little voice in our head that will keep whispering negative things. That little voice in your head could be telling you that you will not graduate from your course because you are not good enough. It could even be reminding you over and over again about how you have failed in the past. Or when the midterm exams are just around the corner, it could keep on telling you to just ditch studying because you are never going to pass the exam anyway. When we give in to that little voice, chances are we are doing things that could greatly affect both our confidence level and our studies too.

Whenever that little voice is telling you all this nonsense, do not listen to it. If you can shut it off then you would be better off without it. As soon as you notice that the negative train of thoughts are on its way, tell it to stop. Do not let yourself be affected by this. What you should do instead is to recall the achievements and successes that you have accomplished before you started college. Do you remember how well you've done in football games? Or how about when you won a debate at school?

If you are to continue excelling in college, you need to ignore that little voice in your head. Don't let it convince you that you are not good enough to be in college or that you do not have the skills. Remember that you took an entrance exam which you have successfully passed. If you were not good enough, do you think that the school would have allowed you to enroll in the first place?

Section 2: Realize That You Are Not Alone

Yes, it is easy to feel lost, left out, alienated and alone when you are just starting out in college. The chances of feeling this way is even greater when you are enrolling in a college or university without any of your friends with you or if you are in a completely new environment. Unlike high school where there are only a few new faces added to your batch every year, starting college is totally different. You will meet new faces regularly and you have a new place to get used to.

That feeling of uncertainty and lack of familiarity might make you feel like you are not good enough or that you cannot do this new thing at all. But hold off on that thought. You may think you are alone. But did you realize that you are not the only freshman in college who feels that way? In this sense, you are part of a group of people who thinks they are alone. And remember, even your friends back home are probably experiencing the same thing.

So what should you do? Start making new friends so you'll have people to hang out with in between classes and after classes. This should help boost your confidence and you can also avoid dreading going to school every day. Every now and then you should also be in touch with people from your previous school to lessen that feeling of loneliness.

Section 3: Choose What You Are Good At

When you choose the course that you will be taking for college, it is really important that you select one that you are good at or something that you are interested in. When you take a course that does not interest you, it is hard to muster up the interest or motivation to sit through long lectures regularly which could eventually cause you to drop out. Do not choose a course that you want to get a degree in just because it is the trend today, it is what others tell you to take or what your friends are taking. Yes, it is fun to do things with your best friends, including being in the same college and studying for the same course.

The same thing is also applicable for the subjects that you sign up for in a semester. Yes, there are subjects that you are required to take, especially the majors. However, you should allow yourself to have at least one subject that you know you will be able to enjoy like an art class or a literature subject. It really depends on where your interest lies. Taking too many major classes in one semester is not good for you either. Major classes require a lot from you and having too many in one semester can be overwhelming. It is easy to feel drained. It might even cause you to fall behind in your classes and it lowers your confidence too.

For the reasons that have been stated, it is really important that you choose courses that you are interested in, something you are good at or ones that you know you can enjoy.

Section 4: Overcome Your Fears

One thing that can hinder anybody from becoming truly confident is the feeling of fear or anxiety. Many fear rejection while some fear being ridiculed. The list of fears that every student has widely varies. So what can you do about this?

You do not have to take big steps in order to overcome the fear that you have. Instead, opt to take tiny steps which will slowly build up the sense of security that you have. Have you always been afraid to speak out and ask questions? What are the different ways that you can try to help you overcome this fear? If speaking in front of the class is too much for you to take as a first step, what you could do instead is to approach your professor after class and ask them any questions that you might have about the lecture. Once you are able to overcome this, you could try participating in group discussions during class activities until you eventually gather the courage to finally speak up or participate in class discussions. What's important is that you start out with things that have the lowest risk for you and slowly build up from there.

Another thing that you can also try out is to do something every day which you consider to be scary or something that makes you anxious. It is not going to be an easy task but if you persevere, you will be able to do it. Doing this on a regular basis and succeeding in it will make you realize that the fear that you have is actually much worse than the situation itself. It will also help you see that though a situation might be difficult for you or that there is that fear involved in it, you can always succeed if you believe you can.

Section 5: Reward and Enjoy Your Achievements

So you've been spending weeks or even days studying for an exam. You now got the results back and you are delighted to see that all your hard work has resulted into something positive. What does this mean? This calls for a celebration. Well, we don't really mean throwing a party and all that. But instead, allow yourself to indulge in something that you know you will enjoy or something that you have had to miss out on in the last few days because you had to study. Buy yourself that slice of pizza that you've been craving for last night but were unable to buy because you did not have the time to go out and buy one. Or how about a nice massage to ease the muscles and soothe you?

Rewards or positive reinforcement should not only be applicable for major achievements like passing exams. You should also reward yourself even for the small things that you have accomplished like keeping your dorm room organized or being able to wake up early in the morning to get to your first class. And rewards do not only come in material things. Giving yourself a pat on the back or telling yourself that you did a great job is also a good way to provide positive reinforcement. What's important is that you acknowledge a success that you have had and savor this achievement.

Why is it good to provide positive reinforcement? For starters, you will find it easier to do the same thing the next time because you have already seen that this action can lead to an achievement.

Section 6: Attendance Is A Must

It is really important that you show up in class everyday unless you are too sick to make it to class. When you are absent from class too often, you will be missing some of the lectures that the professor has provided. When you miss the lectures, you are lacking some of the knowledge that your classmates have because they have always been attending classes. When you do not understand or know certain lectures, it is also easy for to have a hard time following the other discussions. So what does this result into? Not only will you start to perform poorly in class but your confidence level will also start going down because you will start feeling inadequate.

So what can you do in order to make sure that you are able to make it to class daily? You need to keep your body healthy so that you won't get sick too often. For a body to be healthy, you need to have the right amount of sleep every day and eat a balanced diet. Exercising will also be good for you. If you happen to be a heavy sleeper, you could ask your roommate if you have one to wake you up. Or you could set an alarm and set consecutive ones if necessary. Avoid staying up too late on school nights too.

When you do miss out on some of your classes for one reason or another, make sure that you catch up. Ask any of your classmates or even your professor for the topics you have missed so that you can do some research on it. This way you won't feel too clueless when you get back in class.

Section 7: Opt For Small Size Classes

When you are afraid of the possibility of a teacher calling on you to answer a question or two based on a discussion or assignment, your first choice would naturally be to opt for classes that are larger. I mean why not? It is much easier to remain anonymous and hide when there are so many students in a class. The chances that the teacher will ask you questions are lower compared to being in a class with a smaller size.

However, being in a class that's smaller in size will be better for you. First of all, you will have more opportunities to overcome that fear that you have when it comes to participating in class discussions or activities. Smaller classes also have a better environment which is more conducive for learning. When you are part of a small class, you have more chances of being engaged and participating in the discussion. A professor in a smaller class is able to give more attention to their students compared to a professor that has to handle a large class. Because there are fewer students to accommodate, a teacher will be able to answer many of their students inquiries and will have a better chance of tracking the progress for each student. A teacher is also able to have more flexibility when it comes to the teaching approach they will take in class.

Section 8: Get Feedback

One way to get your confidence soaring high is by getting feedback from your professor as early as you can. Many of the students may be afraid to approach professors and some fear the feedback that they might get. But you need to remember that a feedback from your professor is not something that is meant to criticize you. It is a professor's way of helping you move forward and excelling in their subject. If you find yourself being confused about an assignment, a discussion or anything else and need some clarification, then talking to your professor about it is the right way to help you get in the right direction. If you will not ask your professor for feedback especially when you need help, you are only going to make your academic performance and your confidence suffer a terrible blow.

For example, you are doing a research paper that was assigned to you by the professor. You are not quite sure about how it is coming along. You can ask your professor or even a peer to read it for you and give you some feedback. When you ask for feedback, you need to be specific and avoid asking them generic questions. Ask yourself first in which part you need some feedback on. Is it the grammar or the flow of the paper? When you are able to identify which area you need some feedback on then it is easier for you to come up with the correct specific questions so that you can get the right feedback.

When you get feedback from your professor that you do not quite understand then do not hesitate to ask your professor for any further clarification.

Section 9: Turn Mountains Into Hills

Wait, what? We don't mean this literally. But we are trying to say here is if you have any big tasks that you have to accomplish, break it down into smaller tasks so that it will be easier to do. Remember that 20-page research paper that you need to do? Or how about the comprehensive exam that you need to study for which consists of 10 chapters? Overwhelming, isn't it?

When we look at a big task that needs to be accomplished, we start doubting ourselves. Will we be able to accomplish it? Then you slowly start telling yourself that you can't because of this and that. Or when you do try to tackle this mountain of a task, you constantly feel the need to take a break to keep yourself sane because the stress is driving you crazy. And so you decide to take little breaks much often than necessary. When you take your attention away from the task even just for a bit, the mountain suddenly seems much bigger than it was when you walked away. You start feeling even more discouraged and you get an overwhelming feeling about it.

So what should you do to avoid this? When you get a big task, immediately break it down to small pieces. Do not wait any longer because that dreadful feeling that you get from it might overpower you. Identify the different parts of the project or task and assign a level of difficulty to each small task. You should start task that you consider to be the easiest and work your way to the most difficult ones. When you start with the simpler task and accomplish them, you are boosting your confidence because you know you can do it. And you are building a momentum that will help you move forward much faster. Not only will you be getting the task done this way, but you are also boosting your confidence when it comes to accomplishing huge tasks.

Section 10: Practice Before Doing The Real Thing

So you have an exam coming up or maybe a presentation to make in front of a large audience. You cannot help but start worrying. What if you suddenly forget everything that you studied for the exam? Or what if you forget the things you are supposed to say? What if your presentation doesn't go smoothly? And the list of 'what-ifs' goes on and on.

This is quite normal. Things like exams, presentations and other big college stuff can make all of us feel this. Sometimes it is because we think too much of the situation or it could be because we are filled with too much negative thoughts. Continuing with this kind of attitude is not going to do you any good because you are hurting your confidence in the process. So what are you supposed to do?

Remember when you were little and you had to practice before you become quite good at something? Well, the same thing applies for you now. Even though you are all grown up now and in college, it does not mean that you should stop practicing. Like they always say, if you want to be well-prepared for anything then you need to practice. Although there is no assurance that you will get perfect remarks on your exam or your speech will be flawless, at least you will do much better when you practice.

So if you have an exam coming up, ask your study group mates to do a practice exam with you. You can ask each other questions based on the subjects the exam is going to cover. This way you will be able to pinpoint which area you still need to review. Or if it is a presentation that you have coming up soon, maybe you could ask someone you know that will give you an honest feedback to listen to you present. This way you will be able to practice the flow of your speech and feel more comfortable giving your presentation. And as an added bonus, you can ask the person listening to your performance give you honest feedback on what can be improved.

Do not get discouraged when they do give you feedback. You need to remember that it is a way for you to improve and do better. It is not something that is meant to put you down but it meant to be something that is meant to push you forward.

So whatever activities that you have in school, try to practice or do trial runs first before the real thing to help ensure that you will excel.

Section 11: Constructively Take Criticisms

When somebody gives you criticism, it is easy to feel the need to be defensive and give an explanation to bail us out of the criticism. Some even get angry for getting such feedback and even lash out on the person giving the feedback. Or some simply choose to ignore the criticism because they feel like it is biting them. But none of the stated reactions is going to be beneficial for you. Instead, you should start learning how to handle criticisms well. This means looking at it as something that is meant to help you do better academically and something that can boost your confidence although in the beginning it may not feel like it.

So how can you help yourself take criticisms constructively?

- Whatever reaction you are going to initially give upon hearing or sensing criticism should be put to a stop for at least a second. A second might not seem like much but it is ample time for you to process things. The moment you allow your brain to process what is being said, try not to react just yet to the criticism and stay calm.
- Recall the reasons why criticism is good for you. You need to remember that criticism will help point out your weaknesses that need to be worked on. It'll help you perform better too and build a thicker skin.
- So now that you have managed not to react the way you normally would when getting feedback and your mind and emotions are in check, it is time to move on to the next step. Listen carefully to what the person is telling you and do not interrupt him. Try to avoid analyzing the feedback too much and just listen. You also need to remember that the person giving you the feedback might be anxious about what he is doing. It is also possible that the things coming out of their mouth might not exactly be what is on their mind. Nervousness can make you do that so give the person the benefit of the doubt.
- It might be hard to do this but thank the person for giving you the feedback. It does not mean that you are agreeing with them because you are thanking them. What it shows instead is your acknowledgment of your peer or professor's effort to provide a feedback.

- After saying thank you, it is now time for you to process the feedback that you have just gotten from the person. This is your chance to clarify anything that was not clear to you and also share things from your perspective. Do not get into an argument with the person. Instead, try to find out why the person thinks so and what can be done to resolve it.
- If you feel the need to do a follow up discussion about the feedback that you just got, do not hesitate to do so.

Taking criticism positively might be easier said than done, but you need to remember that if you do not receive criticism, you might never be aware of which areas you need to improve on. When you refuse to listen or accept criticism, you might also be missing out on insights that can prove to be useful for you.

Section 12: Learning Is A Process

You need to realize this if you want to be able to keep your confidence level up and continue performing well academically and in other areas of your life. Do not expect yourself to be a master right away at a new skill or subject. It is not something that you will learn overnight. Remember the other skills that you have learned in the past? Try to remember how it felt the first time you tried it out.

Be patient with yourself as you learn something. Do not expect to be able to write a research paper that is going to blow away people right then and there especially when you've never done one before. You are setting a standard for yourself that you have a very slim chance of achieving. Yes, you can write an awesome research paper but it will need to go through thorough reviews first before it turns out to be perfect. Expecting something to be perfect the first time you try it is going to be really bad for your confidence level too.

So again, understand that learning is a process that takes time. There is nothing you won't be able to master if you are diligent enough.

Section 13: Steer Clear Of Bubble Busters

Criticism is one thing and bubble busting is another. A bubble buster is somebody who will be able to find something wrong in what you have achieved no matter how amazing your achievement has been. Bubbles busters can be parents who expect their kids to be perfect in everything and anything less than perfect is not good enough. There are professors as well that have set perfection as a standard. And then there are people who just like to dig up things about you and what you have done. While it is good to accept criticisms, it is also important that you avoid people who keep bursting your bubble. An achievement is an achievement and it is something that you should be able to celebrate. Being around people who always have something to say even about achievements is going to completely hurt your confidence and it might even prevent you from savoring an accomplishment. It is going to make you lose some confidence in your skills.

As much as you can, avoid these naysayers because they are not going to be healthy for your confidence.

Conclusion

Being a college or university student is fun but it can also be stressful. People expect you to act more maturely since it won't be long before you are going to be a part of the real world. Although there are some people who do not feel like college has prepared them for their job, it is still important that you do the best that you can while you are still in college. Many companies look at your college or university grades as one of the basis of whether they should hire you or not during the first job and getting good grades is going to give you a better leverage.

If you want to be able to perform well academically in college, one of the things that you should maintain on a high level is your confidence. Confidence has been associated with performing better in school. A person that is confident is able to tell themself that they can succeed because they have the skills and drive to succeed. A confident person believes in their capabilities. When a confident person encounters a problem, they won't back away from it. Despite the fears that they have, they will still go forward because they know they can and he will succeed.

There are many things that we can do in order to maintain a good confidence level in college. When we get criticism, it is important that we learn how to look at its bright side and when we need help in anything at all, we should learn to overcome our fears of approaching others for help. Getting feedback or help as early as possible is a great way to help clear any confusions that you have about subject matters.

All the tips that have been mentioned in the previous sections can be of great use to anybody who needs a boost in their self-confidence so that they can perform well academically. Hopefully, you will find it useful too. So are you ready to be a confident college student who will excel academically?

EXPERIENCE
EVERYTHING
P U B L I S H I N G

www.ingramcontent.com/pod-product-compliance
Lightning Source LLC
Chambersburg PA
CBHW071812020426
42331CB00008B/2462